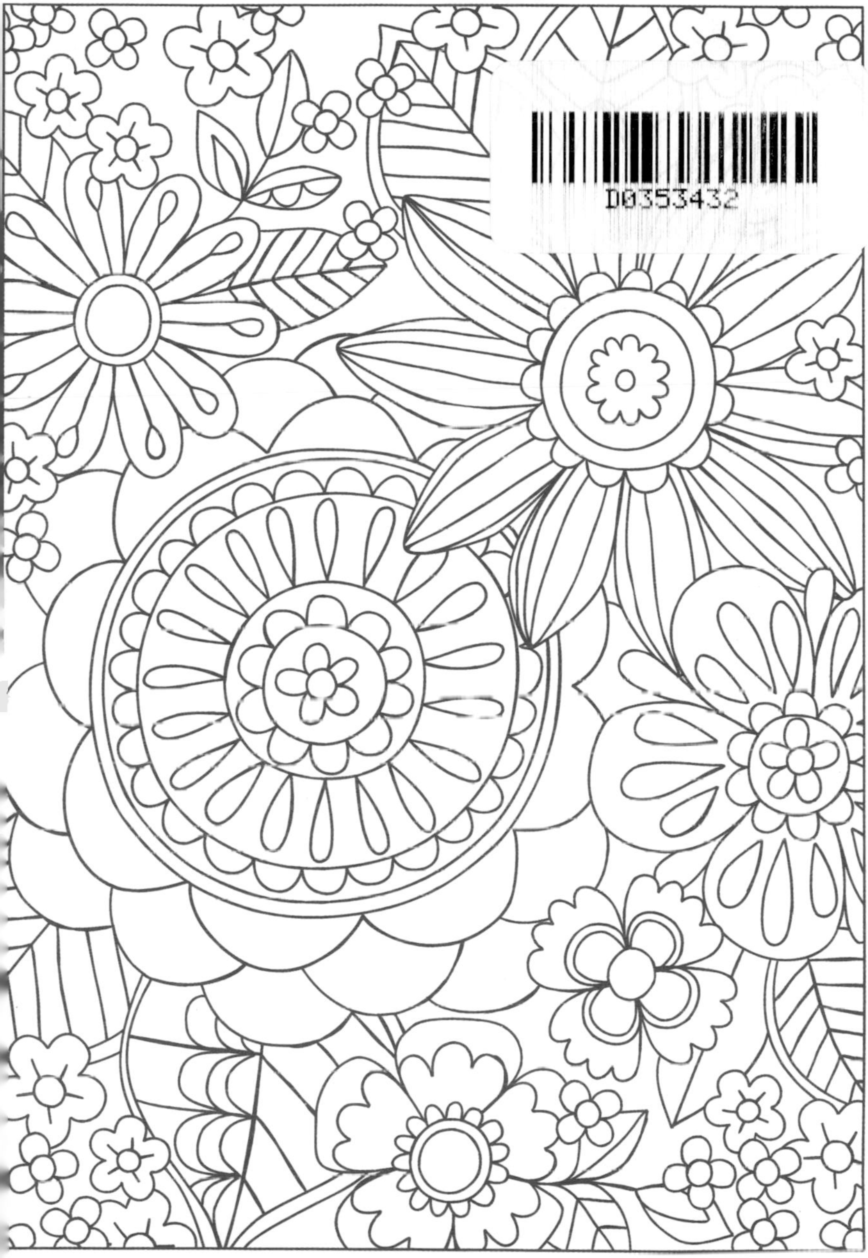

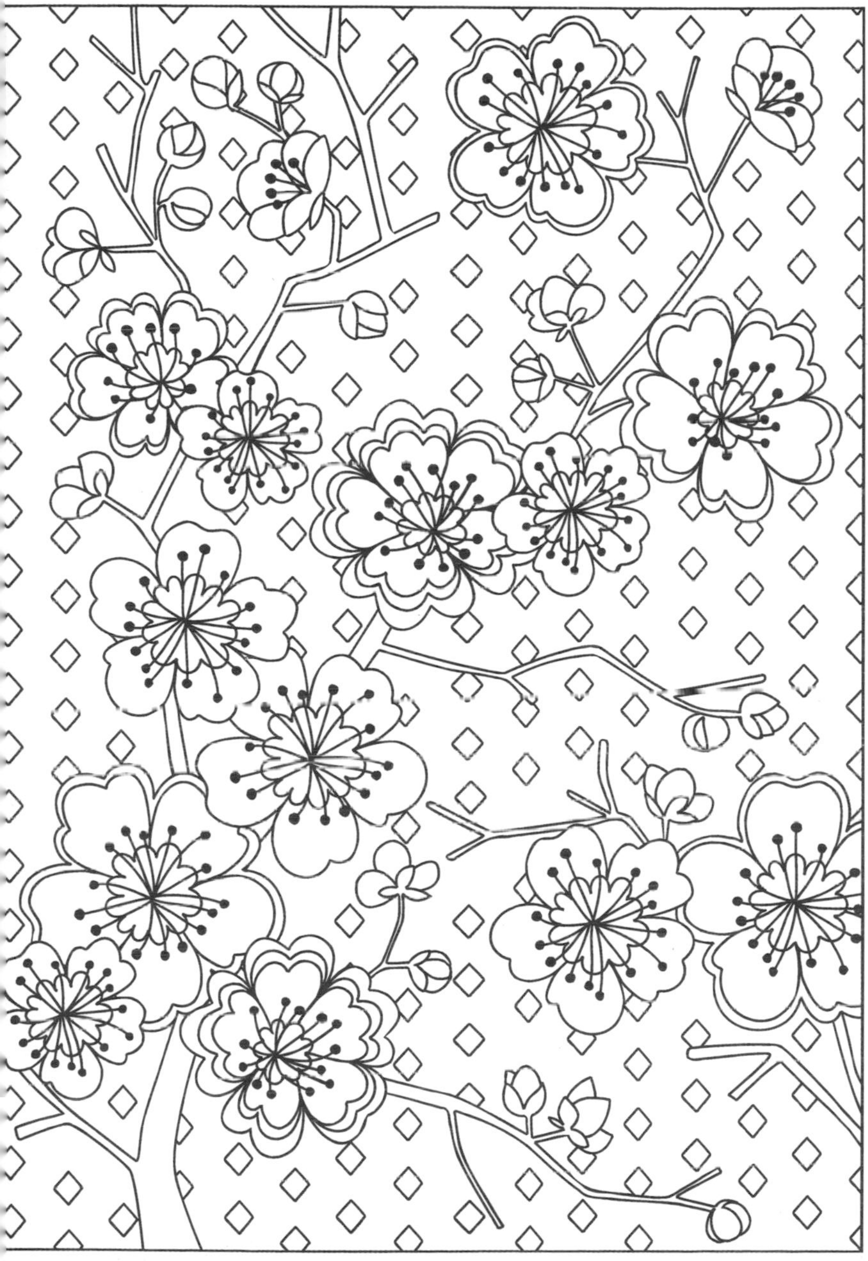

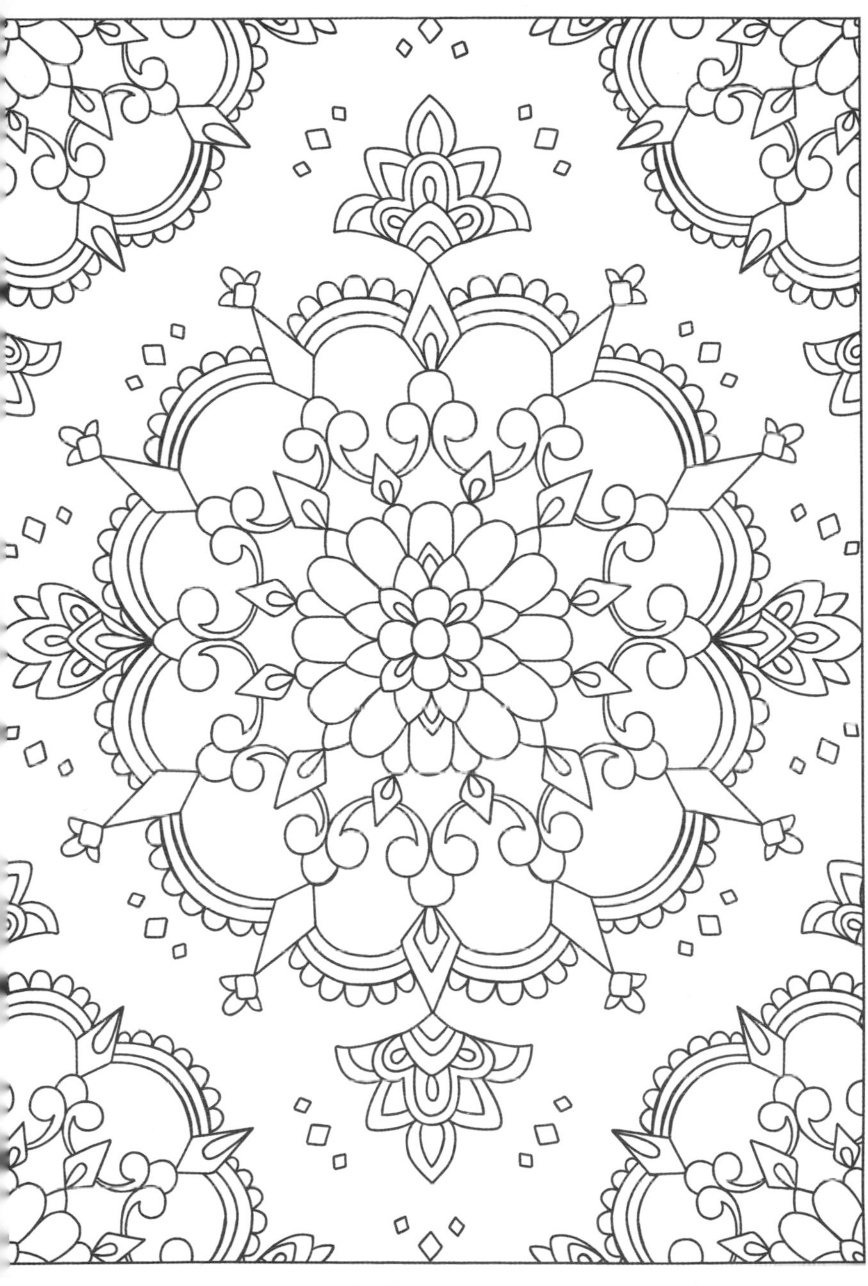

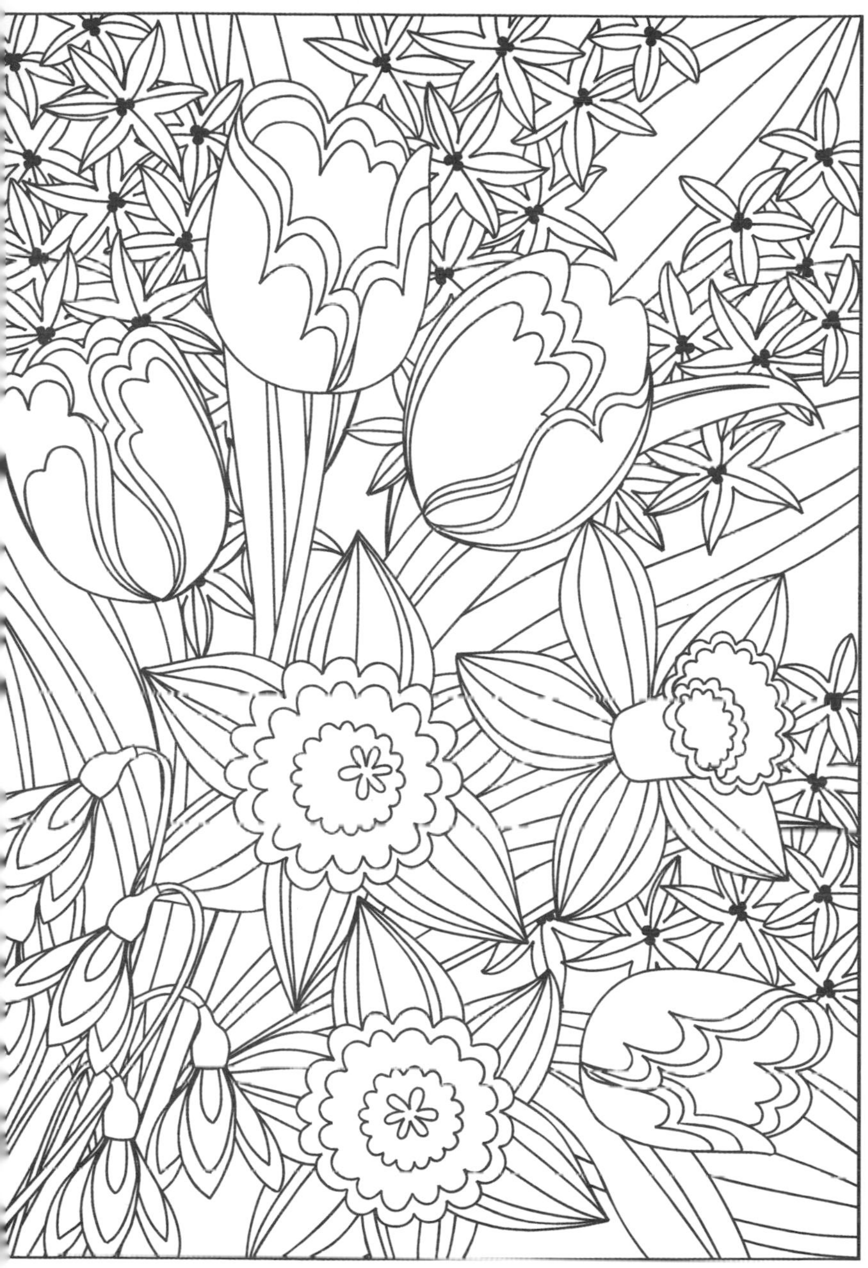

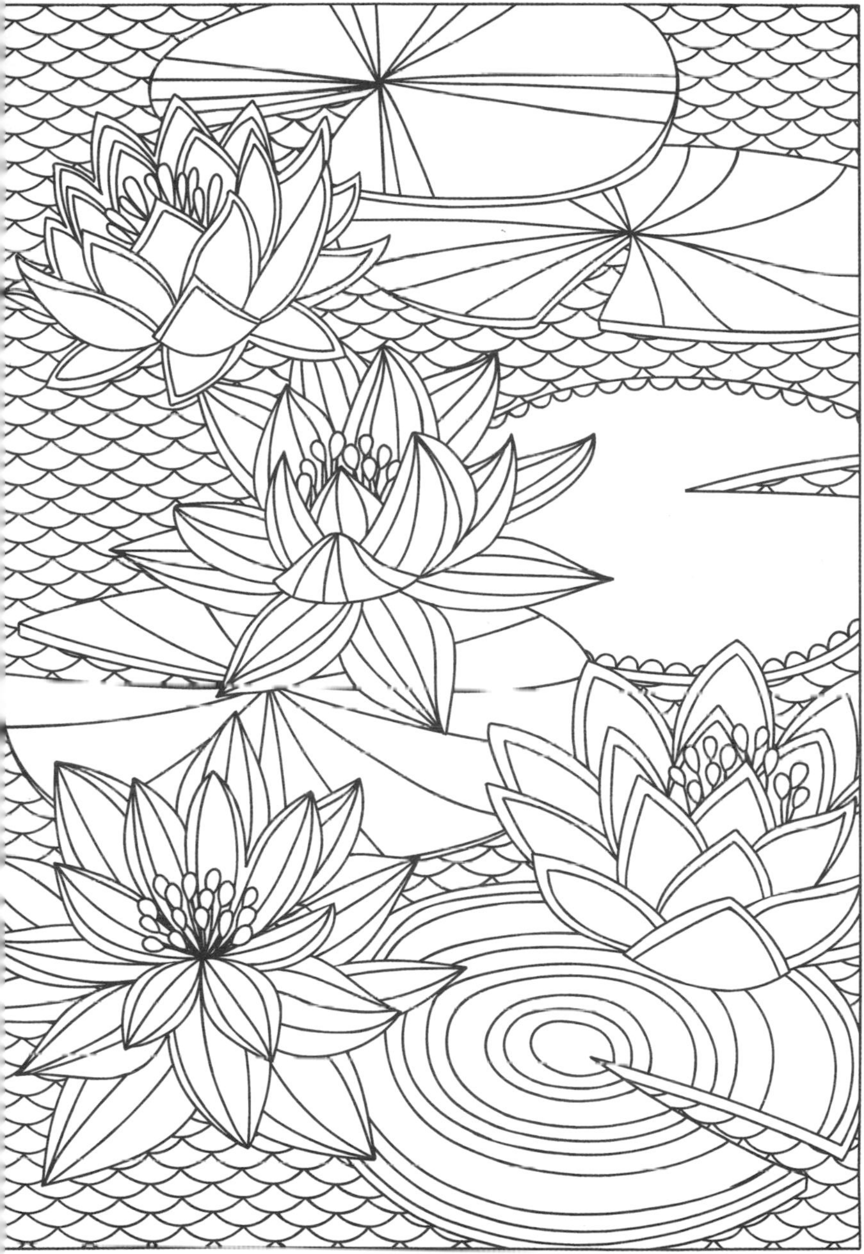

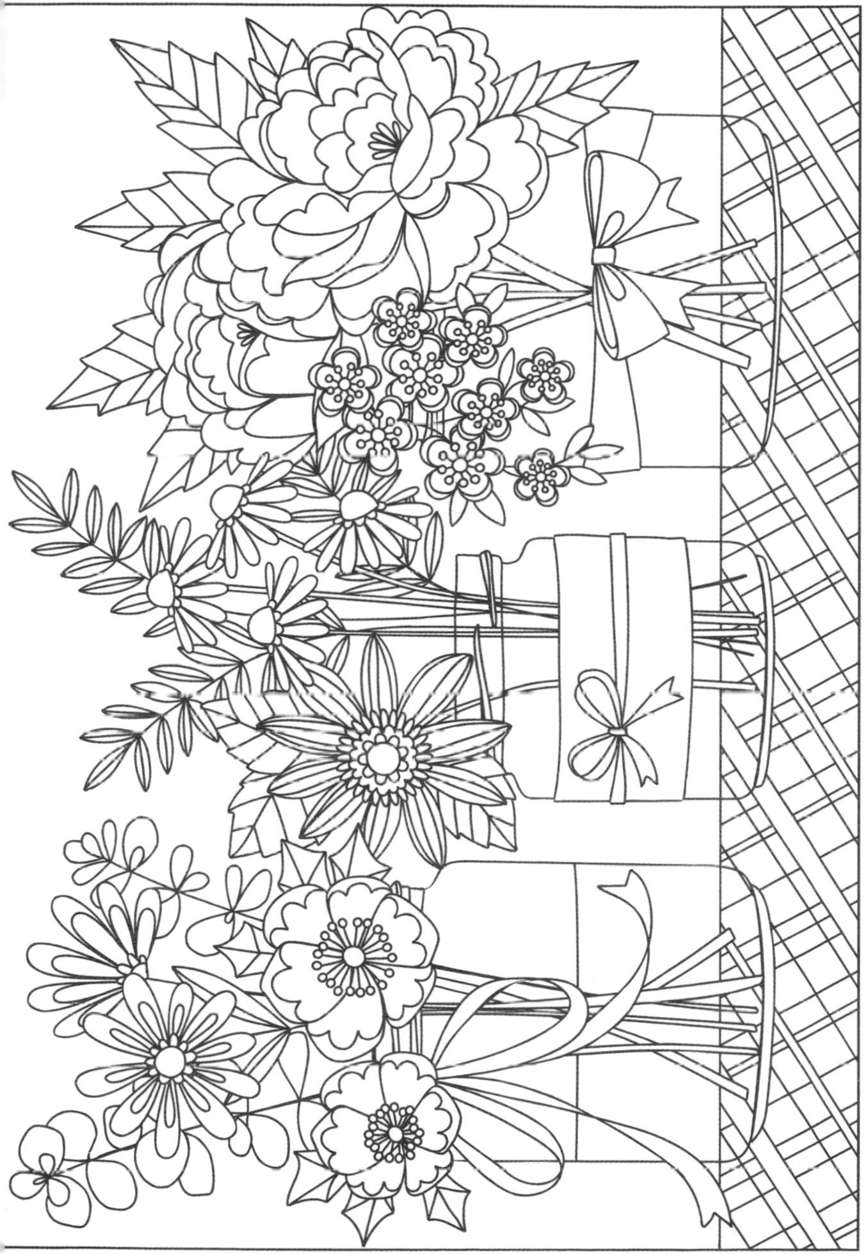

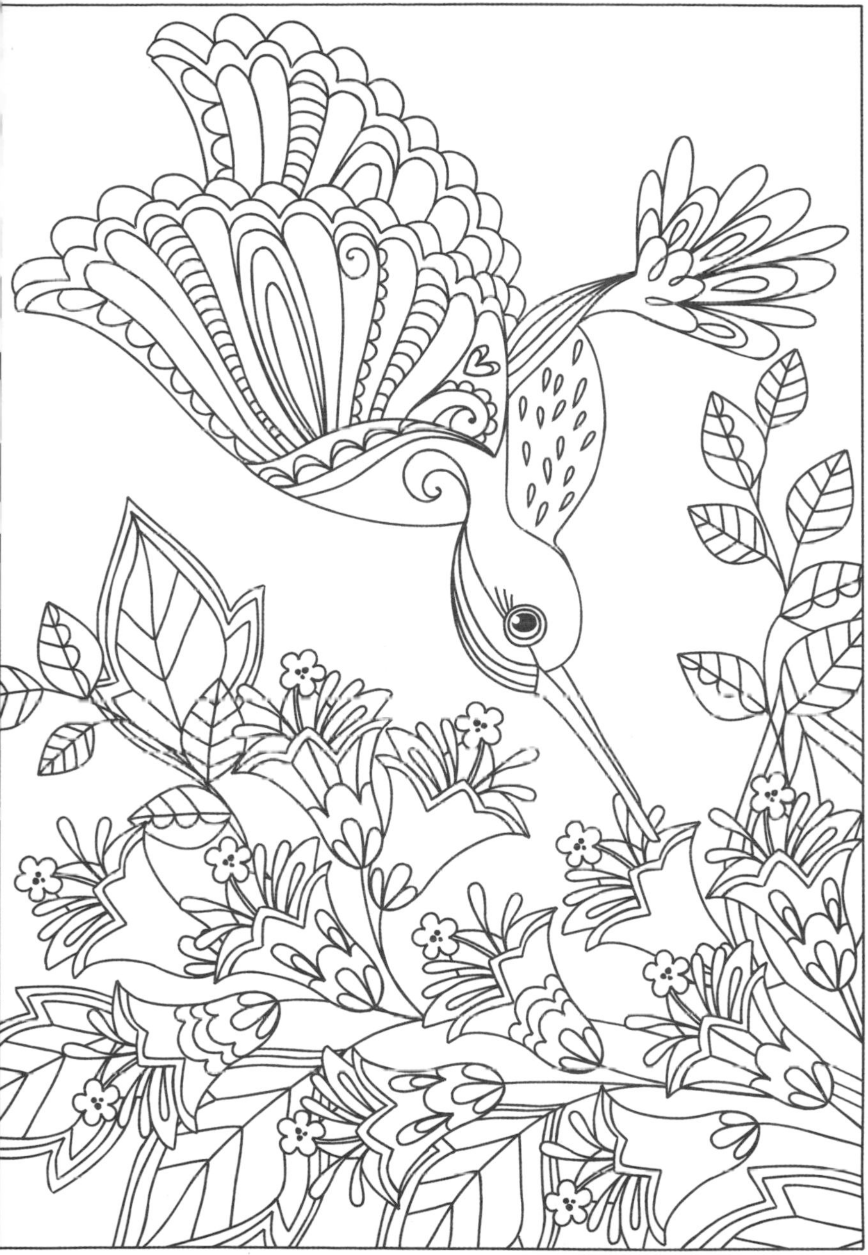

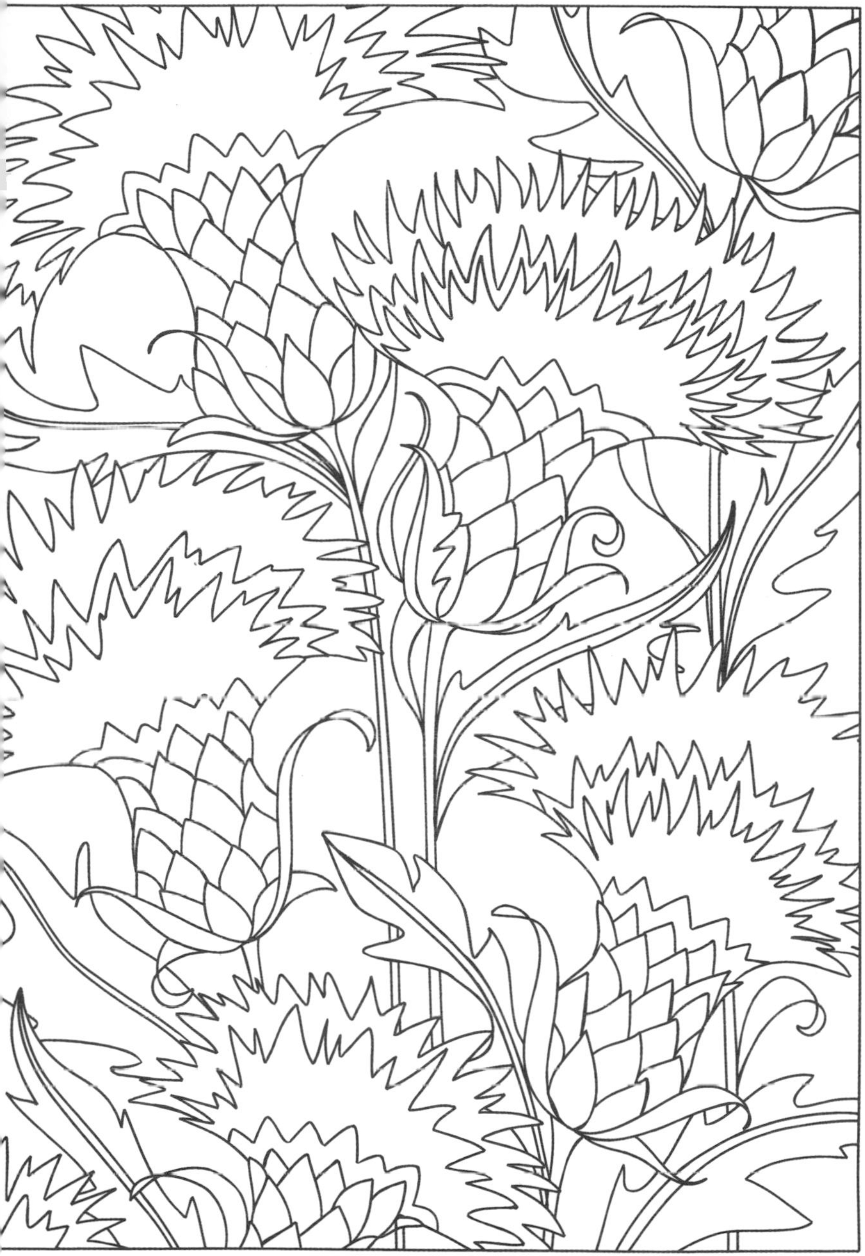

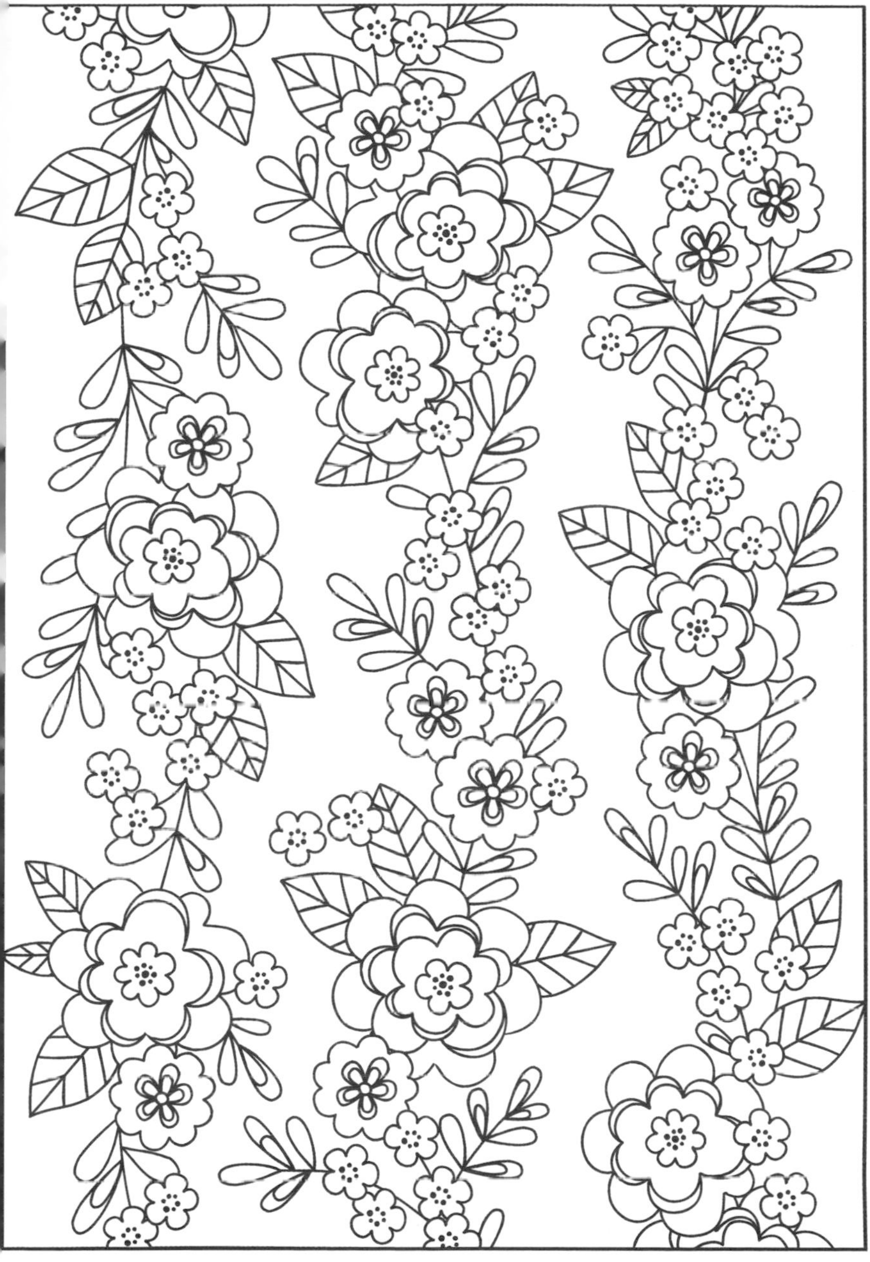

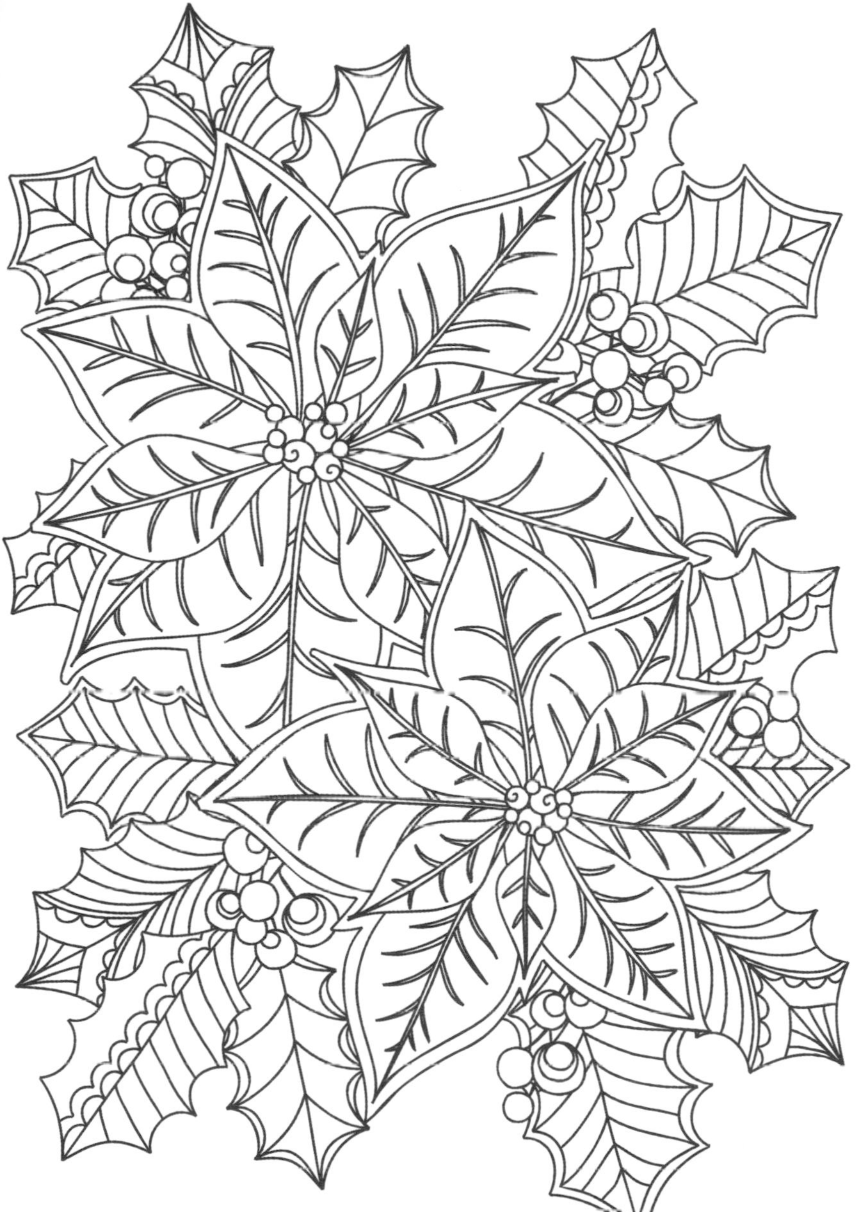

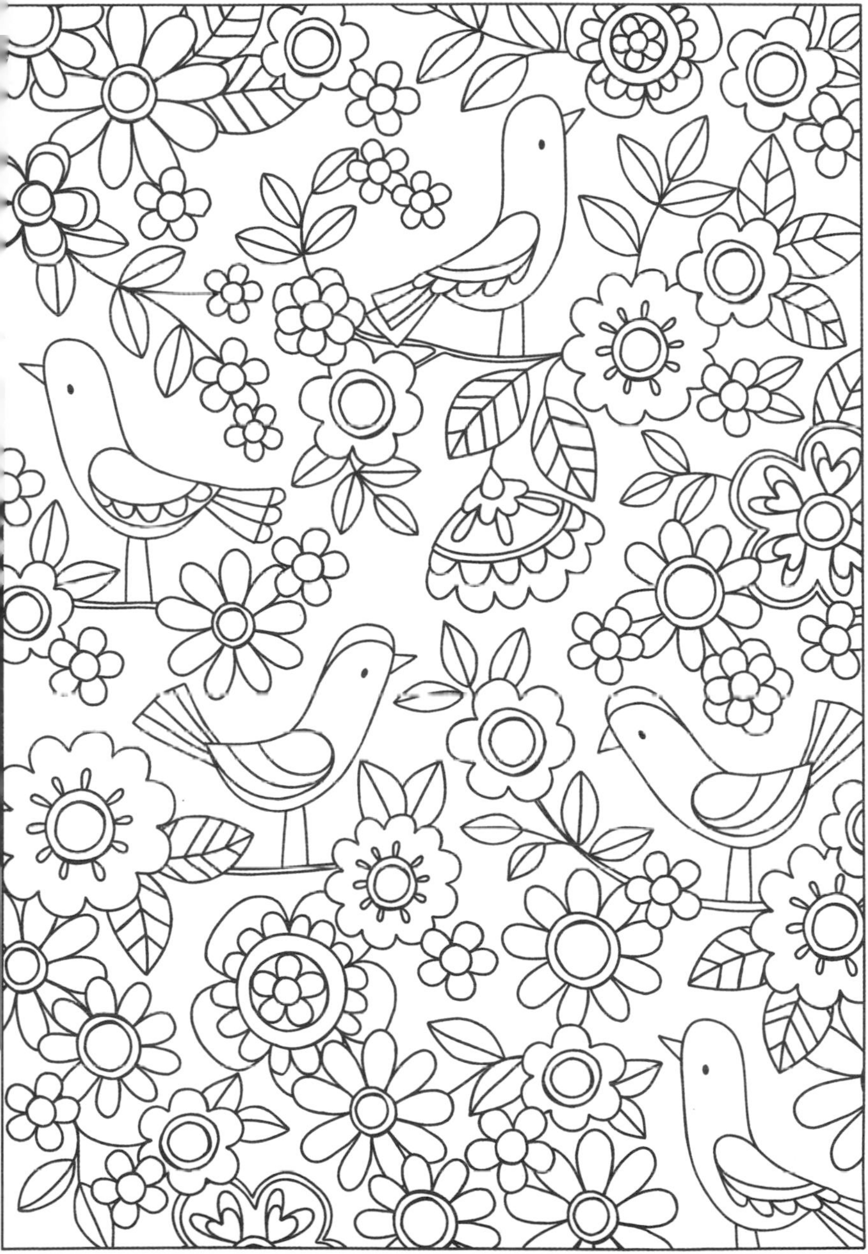

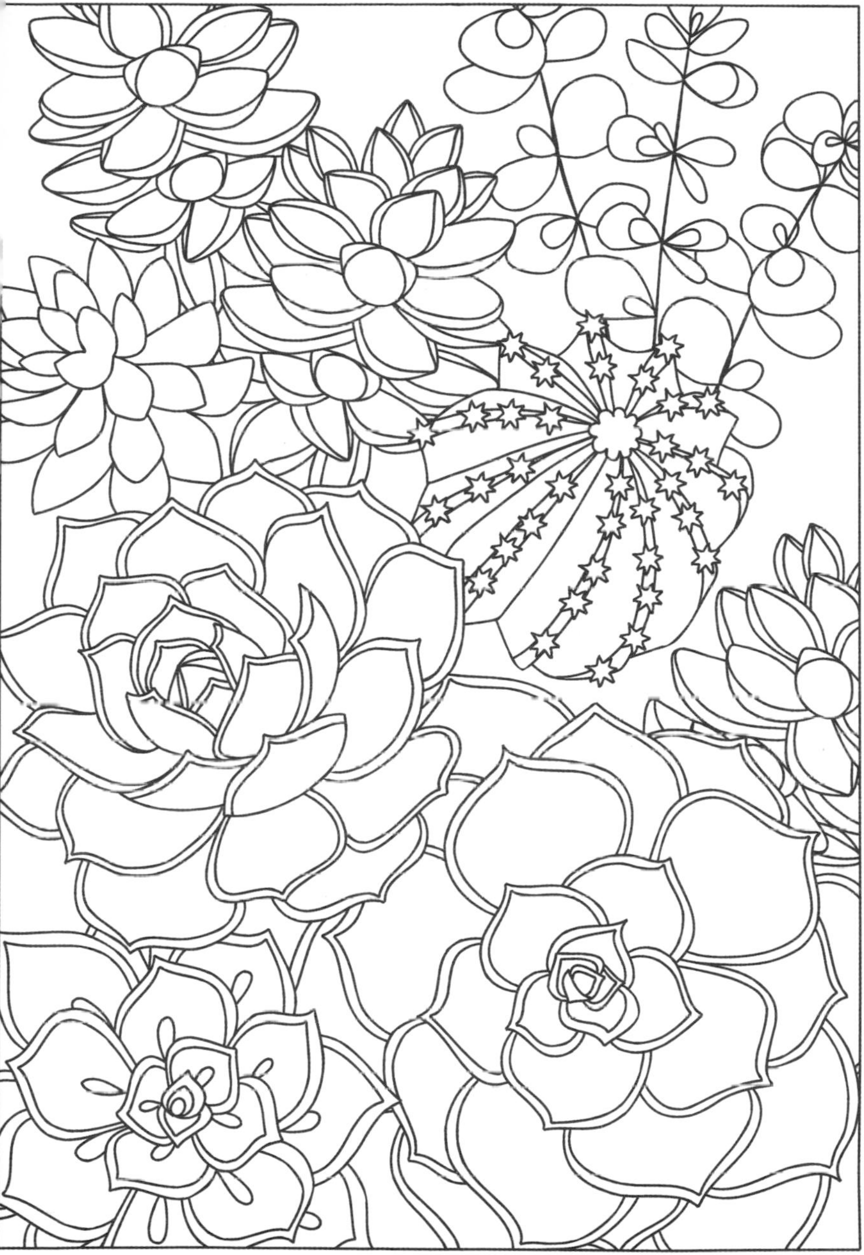

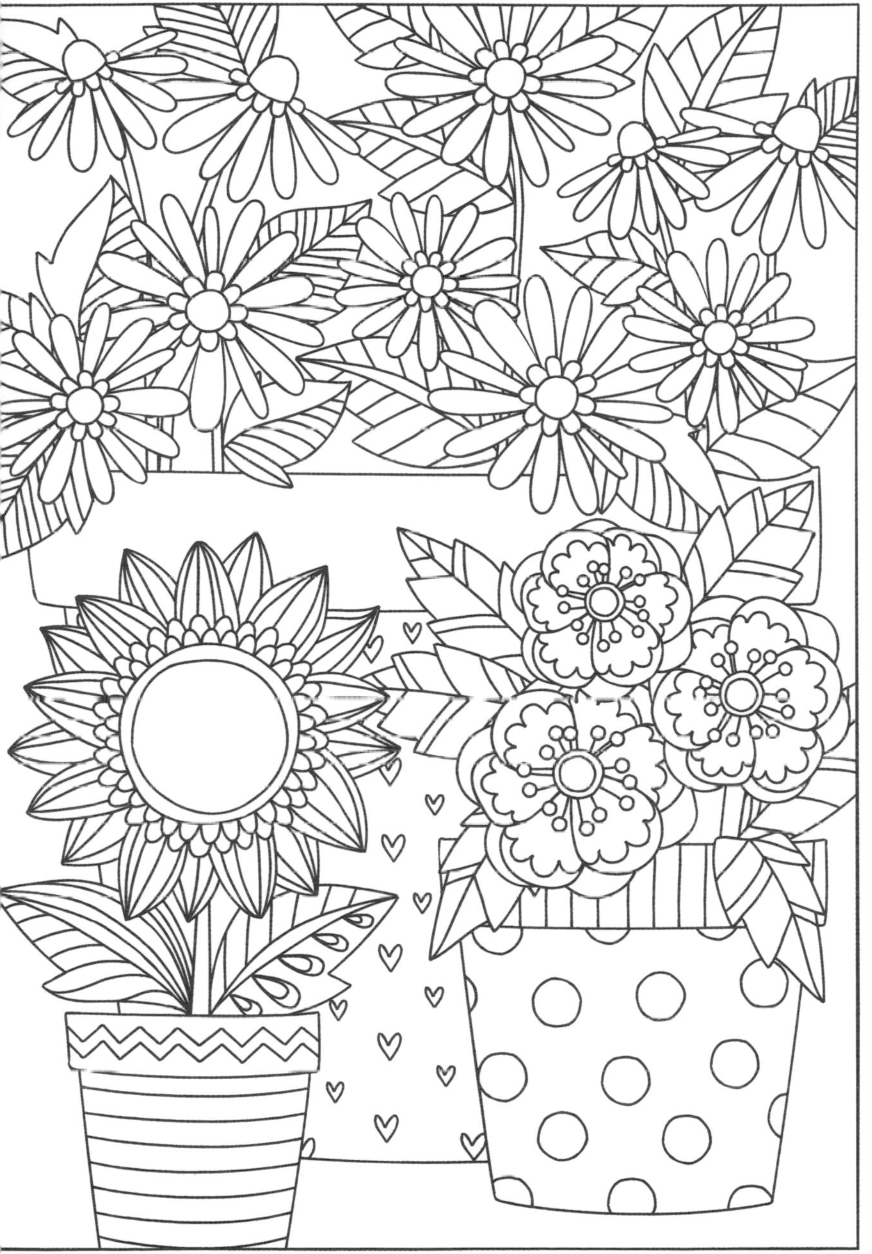

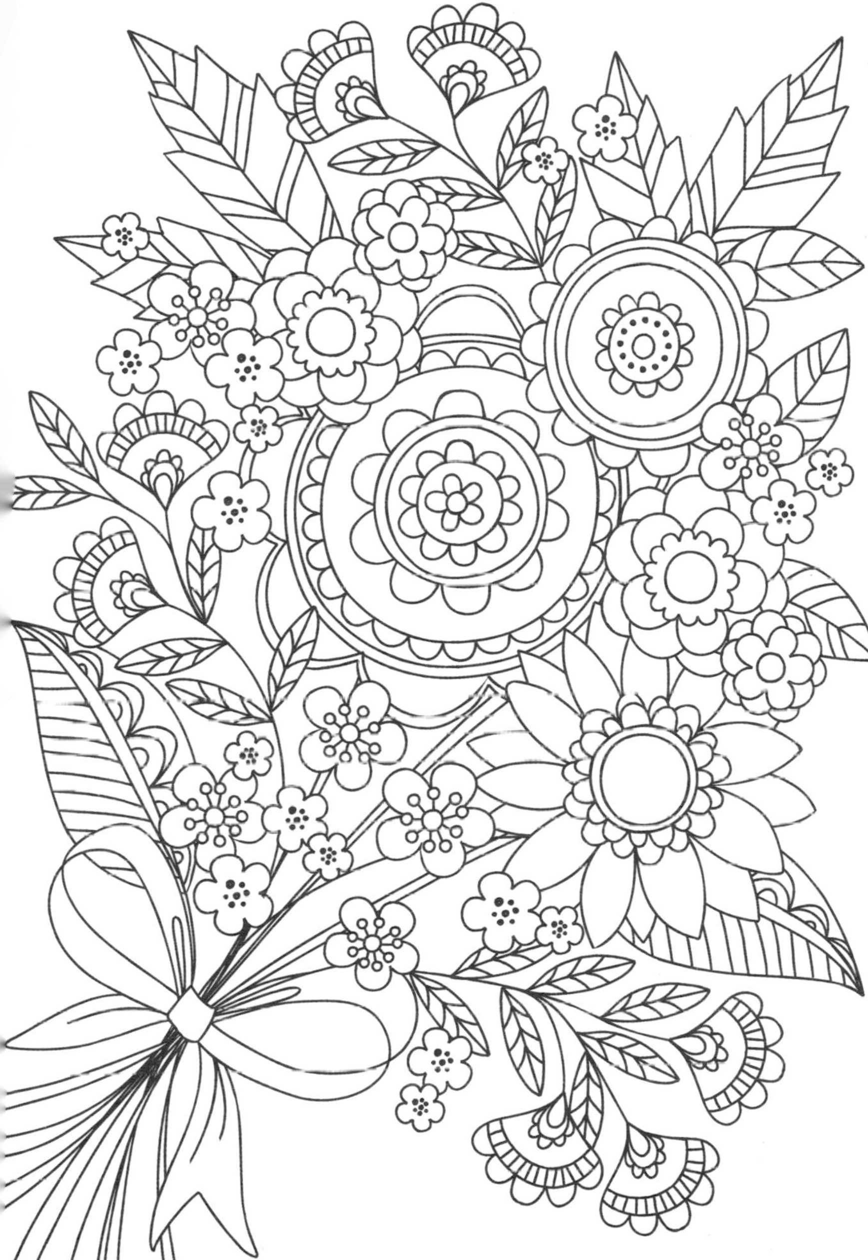

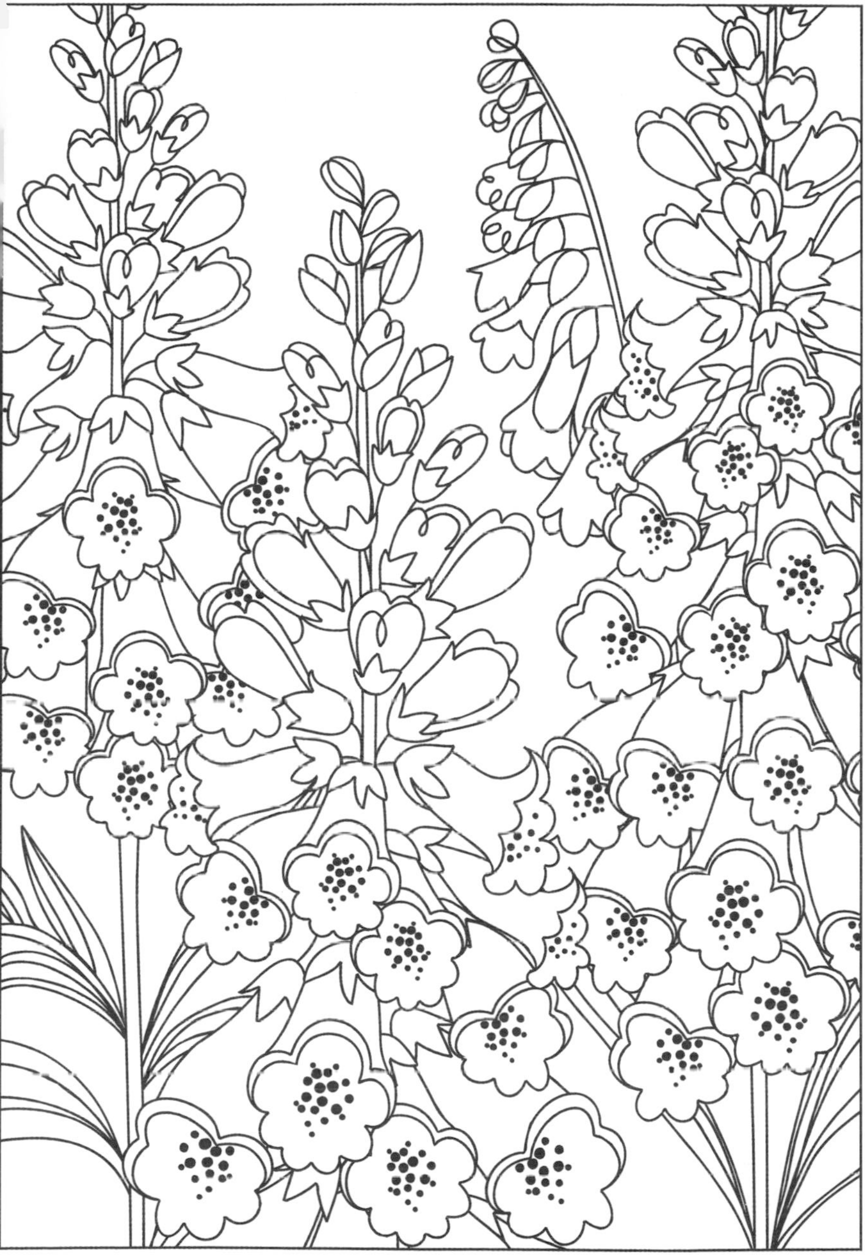

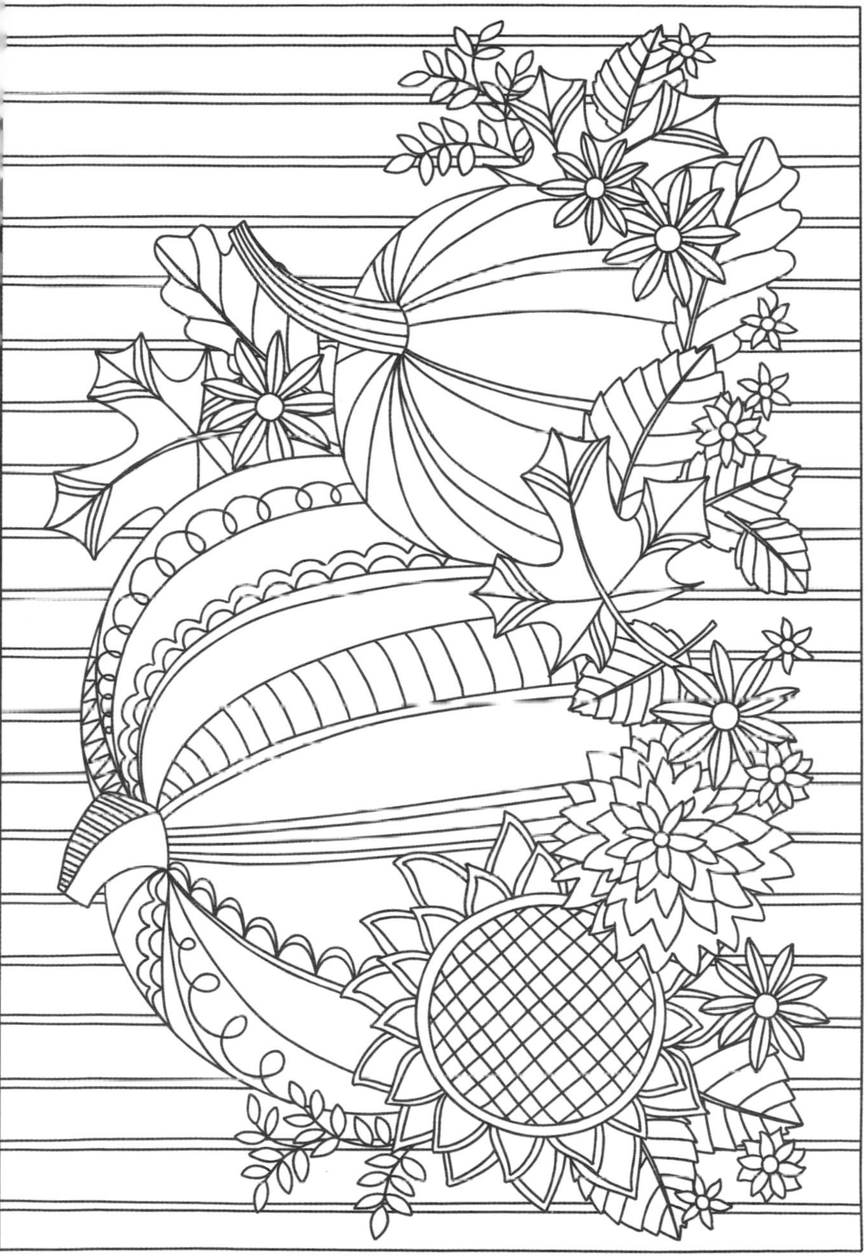

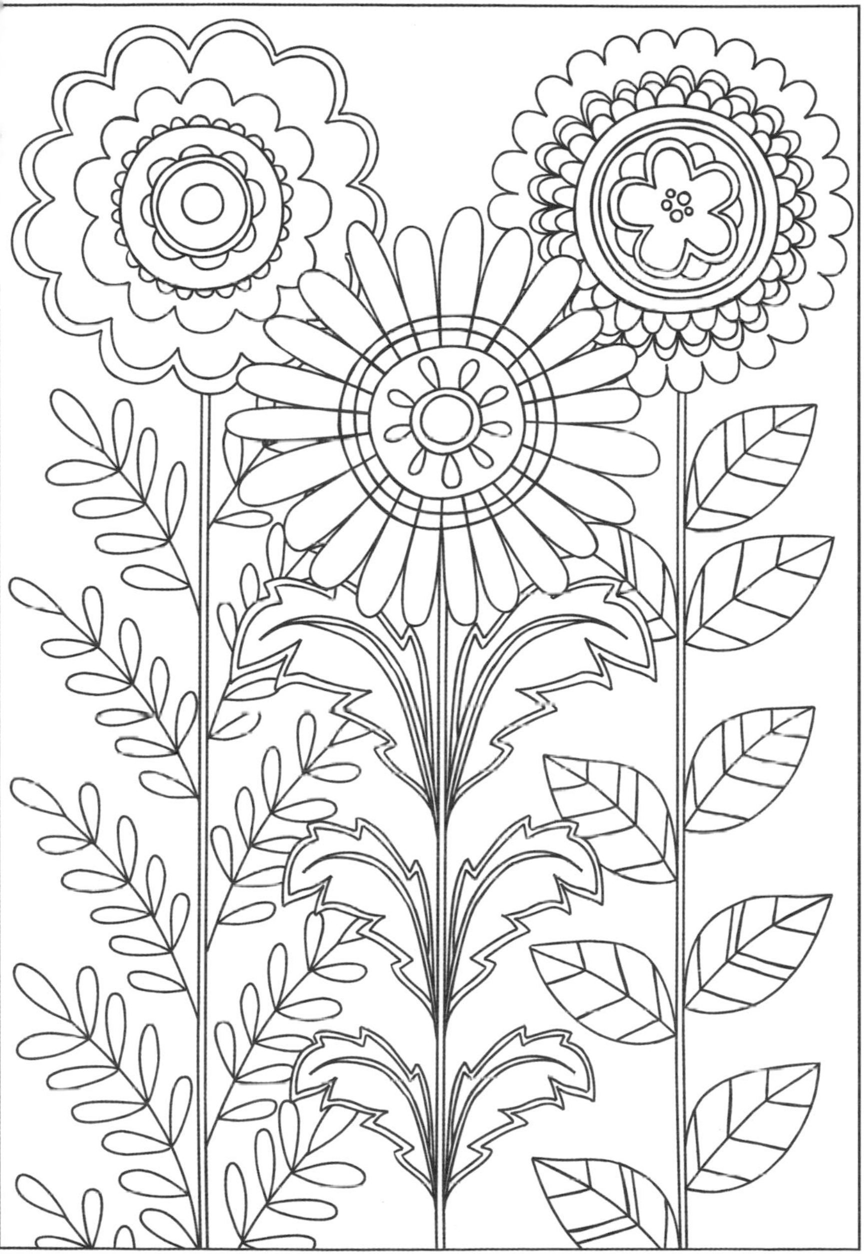

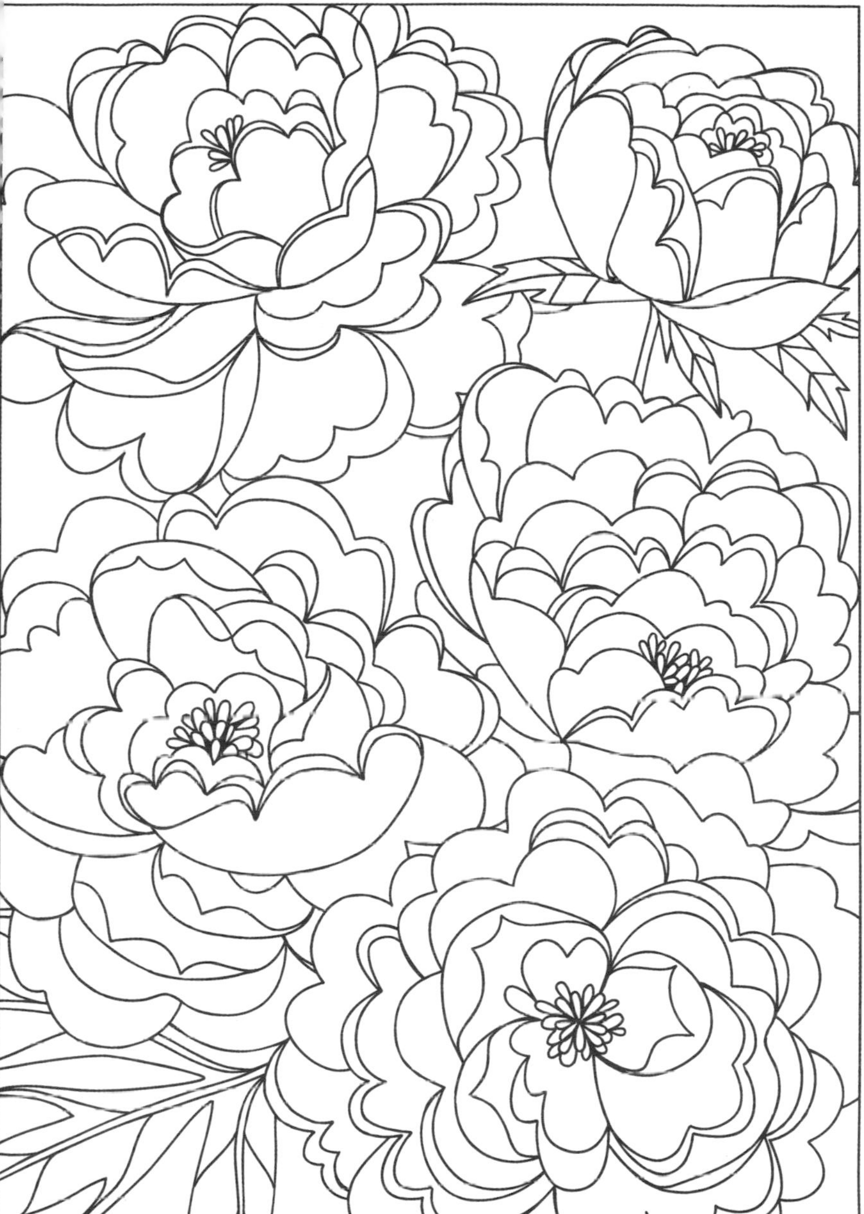

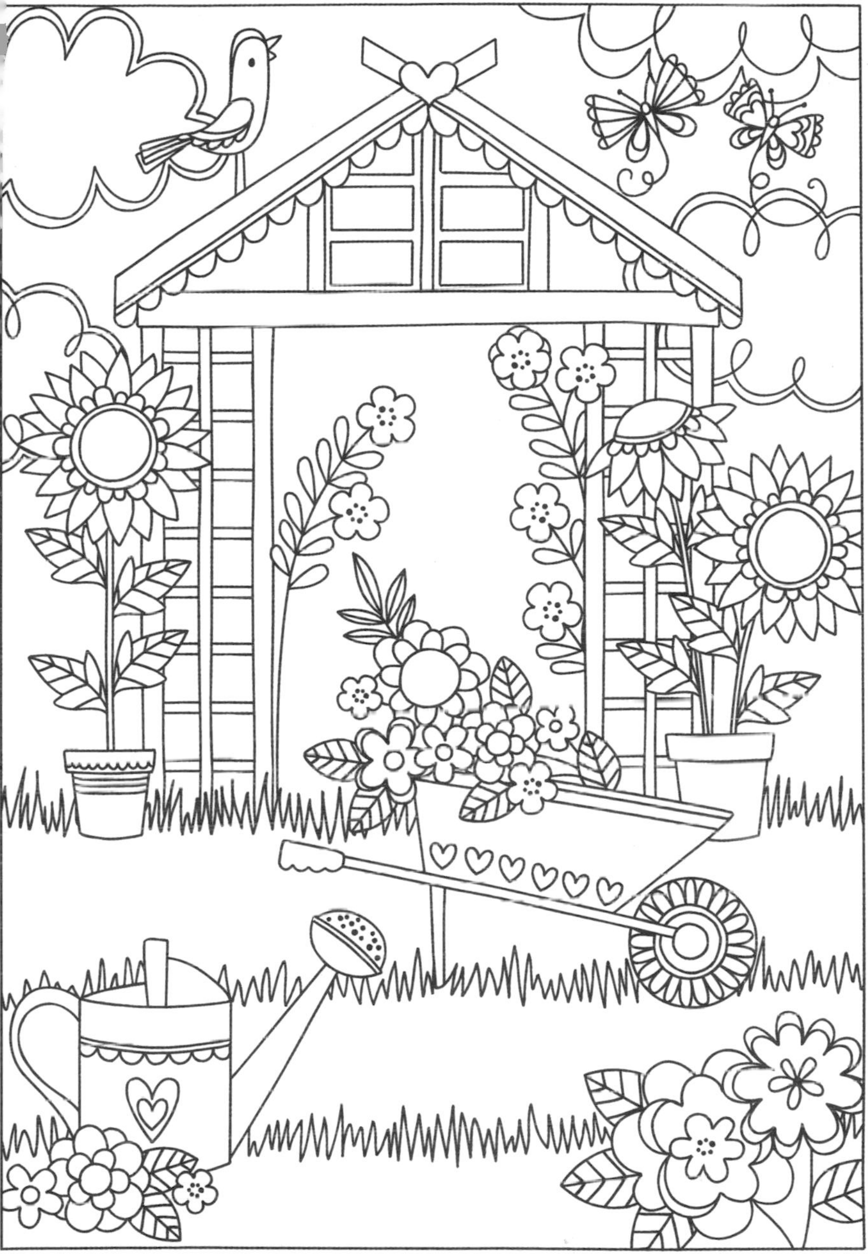